Six Legged World

HOMES AND HABITS OF INSECTS

Lynn M. Stone

The Rourke Book Company, Inc.
Vero Beach, Florida 32964

PHOTO CREDITS
© J. H. "Pete" Carmichael: cover, p. 4, 11, 16;
© James H. Robinson: title page;
© Lynn M. Stone: p. 7, 8, 12, 13, 19, 20;
© James P. Rowan: p. 15

EDITORIAL SERVICES
Janice L. Smith for Penworthy Learning Systems

Library of Congress Cataloging-in-Publication Data

Stone, Lynn M.
    Homes and habits of insects / Lynn M. Stone.
        p. cm. — (Six legged world)
    ISBN 1-55916-310-0
    1. Insects—Behavior—Juvenile literature. 2. Animal defenses—Juvenile
literature. [1. Insects.] I. Title.

QL496 S864 2000
595.7—dc21
                                              00–036931

Printed in the USA

CONTENTS

HABITS OF INSECTS

An insect has two goals in life. The first is to survive, or stay alive. The second goal is just as important. It is to make sure that an insect leaves new members of its kind behind when it dies.

How an insect goes about this business of survival depends upon the **species**, or kind, of insect. Scientists have identified more than 800,000 species of insects. Many of them have very interesting survival habits.

Some insects, called predators, feed on insects which they kill. Here an assassin bug has killed a green bee.

PREDATOR AND PREY

No animal can survive without eating. And no animal can survive if it is eaten. On the whole, insects manage to eat more often than they are eaten. This helps the species survive even if an individual insect is dessert for a bird.

Insects of one kind or another eat a great variety of foods. Many insects, like grasshoppers, eat plant material. Others eat animal material. Finding food is usually easier than staying alive.

Many insects feed on plants, or in the case of this butterfly, on liquids in the flowers.

But insects have several ways to avoid **predators**, the animals that hunt other animals. Some insects simply fly, hop, or race away from danger.

Some insects avoid predators by making themselves look like part of their surroundings. Their color or shape may help them blend in with plants, for example. A predator may not be able to tell the walkingstick insect from a real stick or the leaf insect from a leaf.

Here a plant-eating insect, the grasshopper, has become a meal for the tiny shrew, an insect-eating mammal.

Some insects have very useful and unusual ways of protecting themselves. Stinkbugs are among the insects that give off a bad odor when alarmed. Bombardier beetles fight off predators with a spray.

Bees, wasps, and ants defend themselves by stinging predators. Some caterpillars have hollow hairs loaded with poison.

One insect predator, the assassin bug, falls to a larger insect predator, the praying mantis.

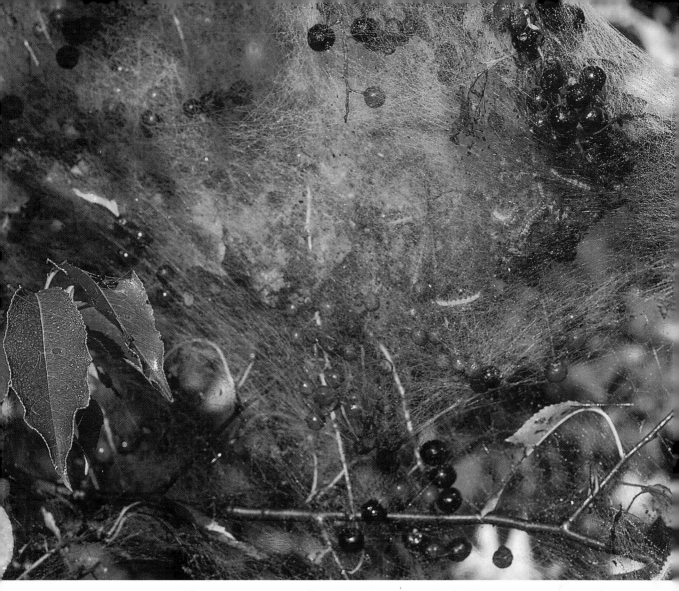

These tent caterpillars live in a "tent" of silky threads they spun on this wild cherry tree.

Termites built this mighty mud mound on a stump in the Northern Territory of Australia.

Monarch butterflies eat the bitter leaves of milkweed. A bird that grabs a bitter-tasting monarch won't repeat its mistake. And that bird won't attack a viceroy butterfly either. Why? Because a viceroy looks like, or **mimics**, the monarch!

Some beetles have long, pinching jaws. Those jaws catch **prey**, the animals the beetles eat. But the jaws also help the beetle defend itself.

Diving beetle larva attacks the larva of a salamander. Larvas are a stage of growth in certain insects and other animals.

TRAVEL AND SLEEP

Many insects survive cold winters by escaping to warmer places. Their travels are called **migrations**.

Migration is unusual among insects. Nature has designed other ways for most insect species to survive. But certain locusts, moths, and butterflies make yearly flights to escape winter.

The most famous insect migration is the monarch butterfly's. Monarchs east of the Rocky Mountains, for example, migrate south in autumn. They fly to mountains near Mexico City.

Monarchs, at the end of migration, spend winter in the mountains of central Mexico.

Winter means cold weather and the end of an insect's food supply. Monarchs fly away from winter. Some insects **hibernate** to survive winter.

Animals that hibernate go into a deep sleep. Their body systems, such as breathing, nearly stop. Hibernating animals use little energy so they don't need to eat. They wake up and become active in spring.

Still as the stone wall of this Iowa cave, a moth hibernates winter away.

INSECT HOMES

Insects often live among leaves, on tree bark, or under roots and logs. But some species live in nests or homes that they build.

Some termites build little towers of mud. Tent caterpillars live in "tents" made of silky material.

Several moths spin silk homes called **cocoons**. Each cocoon is like a tight, waterproof sleeping bag for the moth **pupa** inside. The pupa is one of the life stages many insects go through.

Paper wasps built this basketball-sized nest in Montana.

Wasps can't read paper, but some of them can make it. A wasp produces paper by chewing bits of plants or old wood into a liquid. The liquid dries into thin layers of paper that become a nest.

The spittlebug lives in a home of bubbles that look like spit (see title page picture).

GLOSSARY

cocoon (kuh KOON) — a moth's pupa and its silk covering

hibernate (HI ber nayt) — to enter a deep, sleeplike state during the winter

migration (mi GRAY shun) — a long seasonal journey that certain animals undertake year after year

mimic (MIH mik) — to copy the actions or appearance of another; one who copies another

predator (PRED uh tur) — an animal that hunts and kills other animals for food

prey (PRAY) — an animal that is hunted for food by another animal

pupa (PYOO puh) — the third stage of growth in most insects between larva and adult

species (SPEE sheez) — within a group of closely related animals, such as butterflies, one certain type (**viceroy** butterfly)

FURTHER READING

Find out more about the homes and habits of insects and insects in general with these helpful books and information sites:

- Everts, Tammy and Kalman, Bobbie. *Bugs and Other Insects.* Crabtree, 1994
- Green, Jen. *Learn About Insects.* Lorenz, 1998
- Parker, Steve. *Insects.* Dorling Kindersley, 1992
- Stone, Lynn M. *Animals in Disguise: Invertebrates.* Rourke, 1997

Insects on-line at www.letsfindout.com/bug

Wonderful World of Insects on line at www.insect-world.com

INDEX